Cover Photo by Alan Silfen

ISBN 978-0-7935-2458-7

HAL•LEONARD® CORPORATION

7777 W. BLUEMOUND RD. P.O. BOX 13819 MILWAUKEE, WI 53213

Copyright © 1994 HAL LEONARD CORPORATION
International Copyright Secured   All Rights Reserved

For all works contained herein:
Unauthorized copying, arranging, adapting, recording or public performance is an infringement of copyright.
Infringers are liable under the law.

The Joy Of Life

By Kenny G

© 1992 EMI BLACKWOOD MUSIC INC., KUZU MUSIC, KENNY G MUSIC and HIGH TECH MUSIC
All Rights for KUZU MUSIC Controlled and Administered by EMI BLACKWOOD MUSIC INC.
All Rights Reserved   International Copyright Secured   Used by Permission

Forever In Love

By Kenny G

© 1992 EMI BLACKWOOD MUSIC INC., KUZU MUSIC, KENNY G MUSIC and HIGH TECH MUSIC
All Rights for KUZU MUSIC Controlled and Administered by EMI BLACKWOOD MUSIC INC.
All Rights Reserved   International Copyright Secured   Used by Permission

In The Rain

By Kenny G

© 1992 EMI BLACKWOOD MUSIC INC., KUZU MUSIC, KENNY G MUSIC and HIGH TECH MUSIC
All Rights for KUZU MUSIC Controlled and Administered by EMI BLACKWOOD MUSIC INC.
All Rights Reserved   International Copyright Secured   Used by Permission

14

Sentimental

By Kenny G and Walter Afanasieff

© 1992 EMI BLACKWOOD MUSIC INC., KUZU MUSIC, KENNY G MUSIC, HIGH TECH MUSIC., WB MUSIC CORP. and WALLYWORLD MUSIC
All Rights for KUZU MUSIC Controlled and Administered by EMI BLACKWOOD MUSIC INC.
All rights on behalf of WALLYWORLD MUSIC administered by WB MUSIC CORP.
All Rights Reserved   International Copyright Secured   Used by Permission

18

By The Time This Night Is Over

Words and Music by Michael Bolton, Andy Goldmark and Diane Warren

© 1992 WARNER-TAMERLANE PUBLISHING CORP., MR. BOLTON'S MUSIC INC., WARNER CHAPPELL MUSIC LTD., NEW NONPAREIL MUSIC and REALSONGS
All rights on behalf of MR. BOLTON'S MUSIC INC., WARNER CHAPPELL MUSIC LTD. and NEW NONPAREIL MUSIC administered by WARNER-TAMERLANE PUBLISHING CORP.
All Rights Reserved

End Of The Night

By Kenny G

*Sax melody written an octave higher than sounds.

© 1992 EMI BLACKWOOD MUSIC INC., KUZU MUSIC, KENNY G MUSIC and HIGH TECH MUSIC
All Rights for KUZU MUSIC Controlled and Administered by EMI BLACKWOOD MUSIC INC.
All Rights Reserved International Copyright Secured Used by Permission

30

Alone

By Kenny G

© 1992 EMI BLACKWOOD MUSIC INC., KUZU MUSIC, KENNY G MUSIC and HIGH TECH MUSIC
All Rights for KUZU MUSIC Controlled and Administered by EMI BLACKWOOD MUSIC INC.
All Rights Reserved   International Copyright Secured   Used by Permission

KENNY G
BREATHLESS

SAXOPHONE

Cover Photo by Alan Silfen

ISBN 978-0-7935-2458-7

7777 W. BLUEMOUND RD. P.O. BOX 13819 MILWAUKEE, WI 53213

Copyright © 1994 HAL LEONARD CORPORATION
International Copyright Secured   All Rights Reserved

For all works contained herein:
Unauthorized copying, arranging, adapting, recording or public performance is an infringement of copyright.
Infringers are liable under the law.

KENNY G
BREATHLESS

CONTENTS

Alone

By Kenny G

Bb SOPRANO SAXOPHONE

© 1992 EMI BLACKWOOD MUSIC INC., KUZU MUSIC, KENNY G MUSIC and HIGH TECH MUSIC
All Rights for KUZU MUSIC Controlled and Administered by EMI BLACKWOOD MUSIC INC.
All Rights Reserved   International Copyright Secured   Used by Permission

B♭ Soprano Saxophone

*D.S. al Coda in score

5

B♭ Soprano Saxophone

By The Time This Night Is Over

Words and Music by Michael Bolton, Andy Goldmark and Diane Warren

B♭ SOPRANO SAXOPHONE

© 1992 WARNER-TAMERLANE PUBLISHING CORP., MR. BOLTON'S MUSIC INC., WARNER CHAPPELL MUSIC LTD., NEW NONPAREIL MUSIC and REALSONGS
All rights on behalf of MR. BOLTON'S MUSIC INC., WARNER CHAPPELL MUSIC LTD. and NEW NONPAREIL MUSIC administered by WARNER-TAMERLANE PUBLISHING CORP.
All Rights Reserved

Bb Soprano Saxophone

8

End Of The Night

By Kenny G

Bb TENOR SAXOPHONE

© 1992 EMI BLACKWOOD MUSIC INC., KUZU MUSIC, KENNY G MUSIC and HIGH TECH MUSIC
All Rights for KUZU MUSIC Controlled and Administered by EMI BLACKWOOD MUSIC INC.
All Rights Reserved   International Copyright Secured   Used by Permission

Bb Tenor Saxophone

10

Bb Tenor Saxophone

Sister Rose

By Kenny G and Walter Afanasieff

Bb SOPRANO SAXOPHONE

© 1992 EMI BLACKWOOD MUSIC INC., KUZU MUSIC, KENNY G MUSIC, HIGH TECH MUSIC, WB MUSIC CORP. and WALLYWORLD MUSIC
All Rights for KUZU MUSIC Controlled and Administered by EMI BLACKWOOD MUSIC INC.
All rights on behalf of WALLYWORLD MUSIC administered by WB MUSIC CORP.
All Rights Reserved   International Copyright Secured   Used by Permission

12

B♭ Soprano Saxophone

Bb Soprano Saxophone

Even If My Heart Would Break

By Franne Golde and Adrian Gurvitz

Bb TENOR SAXOPHONE

© 1992 EMI VIRGIN SONGS, INC., CHESCA TUNES, CLASSIC SONGS and WARNER BROS. MUSIC
All Rights for CHESCA TUNES Controlled and Administered by EMI VIRGIN SONGS, INC.
All Rights Reserved   International Copyright Secured   Used by Permission

Forever In Love

By Kenny G

B♭ SOPRANO SAXOPHONE

*D.S. al Coda in score

© 1992 EMI BLACKWOOD MUSIC INC., KUZU MUSIC, KENNY G MUSIC and HIGH TECH MUSIC
All Rights for KUZU MUSIC Controlled and Administered by EMI BLACKWOOD MUSIC INC.
All Rights Reserved   International Copyright Secured   Used by Permission

Bb Soprano Saxophone

*Coda begins in score

G-Bop

By Kenny G, Walter Afanasieff and Dan Shea

Bb SOPRANO SAXOPHONE

© 1992 EMI BLACKWOOD MUSIC INC., KUZU MUSIC, KENNY G MUSIC, HIGH TECH MUSIC, WB MUSIC CORP., WALLYWORLD MUSIC and PICNIC HILL MUSIC
All Rights for KUZU MUSIC Controlled and Administered by EMI BLACKWOOD MUSIC INC.
All rights on behalf of WALLYWORLD MUSIC administered by WB MUSIC CORP.
All Rights Reserved   International Copyright Secured   Used by Permission

19

Homeland

By Kenny G

Bb SOPRANO SAXOPHONE

© 1992 EMI BLACKWOOD MUSIC INC., KUZU MUSIC, KENNY G MUSIC and HIGH TECH MUSIC
All Rights for KUZU MUSIC Controlled and Administered by EMI BLACKWOOD MUSIC INC.
All Rights Reserved   International Copyright Secured   Used by Permission

Bb Soprano Saxophone

*D.S. al Coda in score

In The Rain

By Kenny G

E♭ ALTO SAXOPHONE

* *D.S. al Coda in score*

© 1992 EMI BLACKWOOD MUSIC INC., KUZU MUSIC, KENNY G MUSIC and HIGH TECH MUSIC
All Rights for KUZU MUSIC Controlled and Administered by EMI BLACKWOOD MUSIC INC.
All Rights Reserved   International Copyright Secured   Used by Permission

23

The Joy Of Life

By Kenny G

Bb SOPRANO SAXOPHONE

© 1992 EMI BLACKWOOD MUSIC INC., KUZU MUSIC, KENNY G MUSIC and HIGH TECH MUSIC
All Rights for KUZU MUSIC Controlled and Administered by EMI BLACKWOOD MUSIC INC.
All Rights Reserved   International Copyright Secured   Used by Permission

Bb Soprano Saxophone

* D.S. al Coda in score

Morning

By Kenny G and Walter Afanasieff

Bb SOPRANO SAXOPHONE

Moderately slow (♩ = 74)

© 1992 EMI BLACKWOOD MUSIC INC., KUZU MUSIC, KENNY G MUSIC, HIGH TECH MUSIC, WB MUSIC CORP. and WALLYWORLD MUSIC
All Rights for KUZU MUSIC Controlled and Administered by EMI BLACKWOOD MUSIC INC.
All rights on behalf of WALLYWORLD MUSIC administered by WB MUSIC CORP.
All Rights Reserved   International Copyright Secured   Used by Permission

Bb Soprano Saxophone

Sentimental

By Kenny G and Walter Afanasieff

Bb SOPRANO SAXOPHONE

© 1992 EMI BLACKWOOD MUSIC INC., KUZU MUSIC, KENNY G MUSIC, HIGH TECH MUSIC, WB MUSIC CORP. and WALLYWORLD MUSIC
All Rights for KUZU MUSIC Controlled and Administered by EMI BLACKWOOD MUSIC INC.
All rights on behalf of WALLYWORLD MUSIC administered by WB MUSIC CORP.
All Rights Reserved   International Copyright Secured   Used by Permission

Bb Soprano Saxophone

A Year Ago

By Kenny G

Bb TENOR SAXOPHONE

© 1992 EMI BLACKWOOD MUSIC INC., KUZU MUSIC, KENNY G MUSIC and HIGH TECH MUSIC
All Rights for KUZU MUSIC Controlled and Administered by EMI BLACKWOOD MUSIC INC.
All Rights Reserved   International Copyright Secured   Used by Permission

31

Bb Tenor Saxophone

The Wedding Song

By Kenny G and Walter Afanasieff

B♭ SOPRANO SAXOPHONE

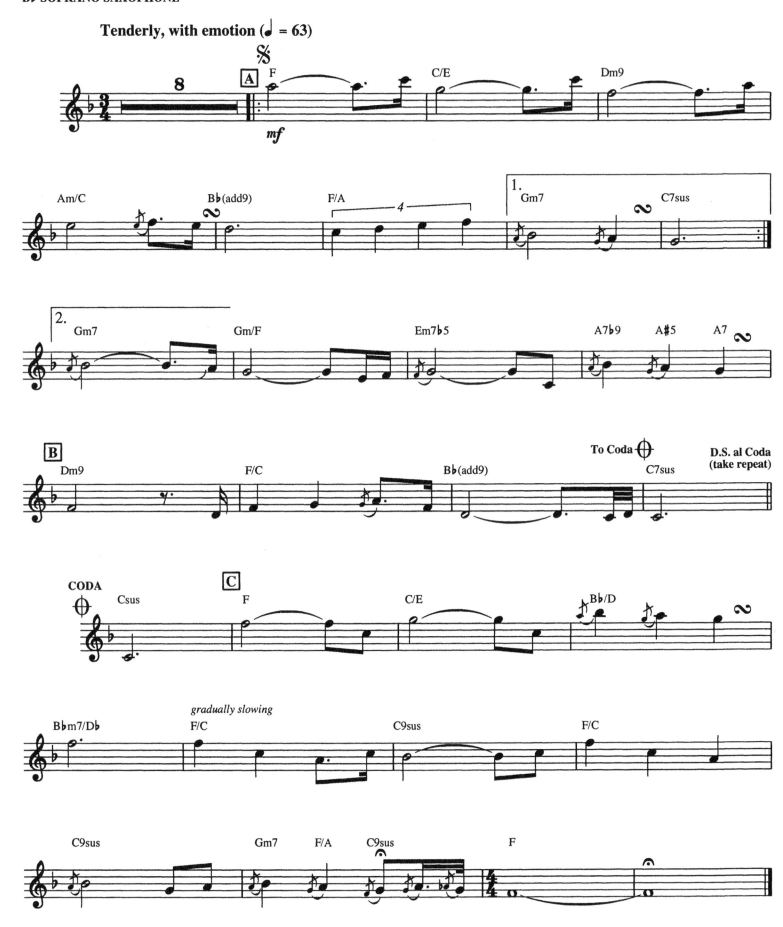

© 1992 EMI BLACKWOOD MUSIC. INC., KUZU MUSIC, KENNY G MUSIC, HIGH TECH MUSIC, WB MUSIC CORP. and WALLYWORLD MUSIC
All Rights for KUZU MUSIC Controlled and Administered by EMI BLACKWOOD MUSIC INC.
All rights on behalf of WALLYWORLD MUSIC administered by WB MUSIC CORP.
All Rights Reserved   International Copyright Secured   Used by Permission

sim. (2 bar pattern)

Morning

By Kenny G and Walter Afanasieff

© 1992 EMI BLACKWOOD MUSIC INC., KUZU MUSIC, KENNY G MUSIC, HIGH TECH MUSIC, WB MUSIC CORP. and WALLYWORLD MUSIC
All Rights for KUZU MUSIC Controlled and Administered by EMI BLACKWOOD MUSIC INC.
All rights on behalf of WALLYWORLD MUSIC administered by WB MUSIC CORP.
All Rights Reserved   International Copyright Secured   Used by Permission

Even If My Heart Would Break

By Franne Golde and Adrian Gurvitz

© 1992 EMI VIRGIN SONGS, INC., CHESCA TUNES, CLASSIC SONGS and WARNER BROS. MUSIC
All Rights for CHESCA TUNES Controlled and Administered by EMI VIRGIN SONGS, INC.
All Rights Reserved   International Copyright Secured   Used by Permission

Vocal
T. Sax
Kybd.
Guitar
Bass
Drums
knew I found heav - en and I've been want - ing to tell you I nev - er wan - na
to a true be - liev - er when you left your trac - es on that
C G Bm7
let you go.
moon - lit night.
B
It may be win - ter in E - den,
but what I'm feel - ing
It may be win - ter in E - den,
but when I'm with you,
2nd time only
D add String Pad
D♯dim
Play both times
(no Snare 2nd time)
sim.
is sum - mer in my heart.
it's sum - mer in my heart.
C
Is it too fa - mil - iar to
(2nd time fill)
Em Csus2 G Em7
Organ
fills
fill
(add Snare)

G-Bop

By Kenny G, Walter Afanasieff and Dan Shea

© 1992 EMI BLACKWOOD MUSIC INC., KUZU MUSIC, KENNY G MUSIC, HIGH TECH MUSIC, WB MUSIC CORP., WALLYWORLD MUSIC and PICNIC HILL MUSIC
All Rights for KUZU MUSIC Controlled and Administered by EMI BLACKWOOD MUSIC INC.
All rights on behalf of WALLYWORLD MUSIC administered by WB MUSIC CORP.
All Rights Reserved   International Copyright Secured   Used by Permission

Sister Rose

By Kenny G and Walter Afanasieff

© 1992 EMI BLACKWOOD MUSIC INC., KUZU MUSIC, KENNY G MUSIC, HIGH TECH MUSIC, WB MUSIC CORP. and WALLYWORLD MUSIC
All Rights for KUZU MUSIC Controlled and Administered by EMI BLACKWOOD MUSIC INC.
All rights on behalf of WALLYWORLD MUSIC administered by WB MUSIC CORP.
All Rights Reserved   International Copyright Secured   Used by Permission

A Year Ago

By Kenny G

© 1992 EMI BLACKWOOD MUSIC INC., KUZU MUSIC, KENNY G MUSIC and HIGH TECH MUSIC
All Rights for KUZU MUSIC Controlled and Administered by EMI BLACKWOOD MUSIC INC.
All Rights Reserved   International Copyright Secured   Used by Permission

Homeland

By Kenny G

© 1992 EMI BLACKWOOD MUSIC INC., KUZU MUSIC, KENNY G MUSIC and HIGH TECH MUSIC
All Rights for KUZU MUSIC Controlled and Administered by EMI BLACKWOOD MUSIC INC.
All Rights Reserved   International Copyright Secured   Used by Permission

68

The Wedding Song

By Kenny G and Walter Afanasieff

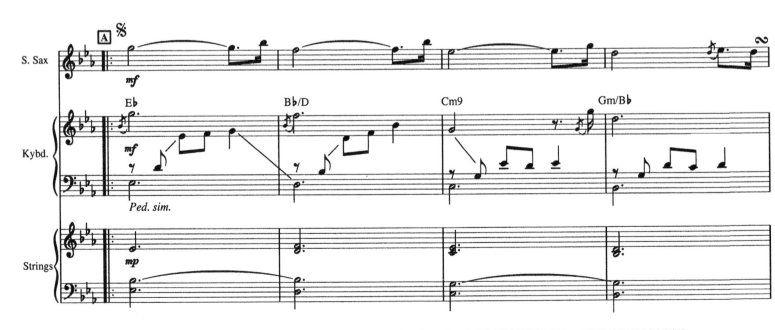

© 1992 EMI BLACKWOOD MUSIC INC., KUZU MUSIC, KENNY G MUSIC, HIGH TECH MUSIC, WB MUSIC CORP. and WALLYWORLD MUSIC
All Rights for KUZU MUSIC Controlled and Administered by EMI BLACKWOOD MUSIC INC.
All rights on behalf of WALLYWORLD MUSIC administered by WB MUSIC CORP.
All Rights Reserved   International Copyright Secured   Used by Permission

Animato ma espansivo

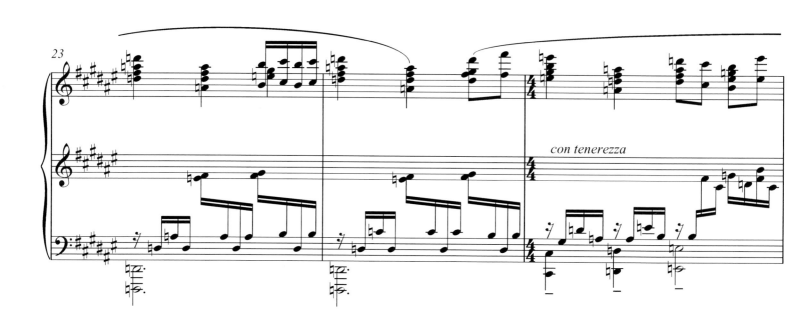

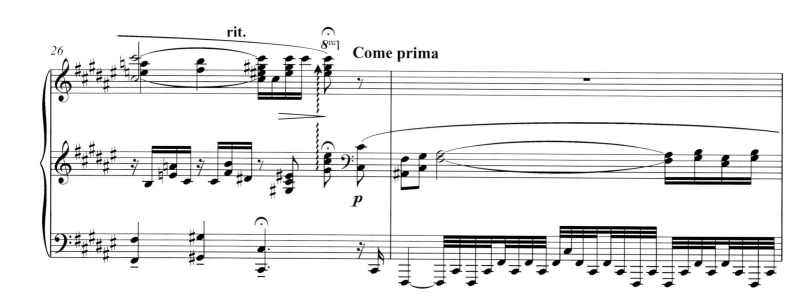